METATEXT

IMMATERIALISM

VILÉM FLUSSER

METAFLUX

IMMATERIALISM

⋆

FIRST PUBLISHED IN PORTUGUESE AS AN ARTICLE IN THE *BOLETIM DA SOCIEDADE BRASILEIRA DE HISTÓRIA DA CIÊNCIA*, 1987

⋆

THIS IS THE AUTHOR'S OWN ENGLISH VERSION.

⋆

⋆

1.PHILOSOPHY 2.POETRY 3.ART

⋆

FIRST EDITION

⋆

ART AND BOOK CONCEPT BY CHAGRIN

⋆

THIS BOOK WAS CREATED WITH COURIER NEW

⋆

PUBLISHED BY METAFLUX PUBLISHING
WWW.METAFLUXPUBLISHING.COM

⋆

DISTRIBUTED BY INGRAM CONTENT GROUP
WWW.INGRAMCONTENT.COM

⋆

ISBN 978-0-9933272-1-6

M
MSM
MSISM
MSILISM
MSILALISM
MSILAIALISM
MSILAIRIALISM
MSILAIRERIALISM
MSILAIRETERIALISM
MSILAIRETATERIALISM
MSILAIRETAMATERIALISM
MSILAIRETAMMMATERIALISM
MSILAIRETAMMIMMATERIALISM
MSILAIRETAMMMATERIALISM
MSILAIRETAMATERIALISM
MSILAIRETATERIALISM
MSILAIRETERIALISM
MSILAIRERIALISM
MSILAIRIALISM
MSILAIALISM
MSILALISM
MSILISM
MSISM
MSM
M

WHATISMIND?NOMATTER
HATISMIND?NOMATTERW
ATISMIND?NOMATTERWH
TISMIND?NOMATTERWHA
ISMIND?NOMATTERWHAT
SMIND?NOMATTERWHATI
MIND?NOMATTERWHATIS
IND?NOMATTERWHATISM
ND?NOMATTERWHATISMI
D?NOMATTERWHATISMIN
?NOMATTERWHATISMIND
NOMATTERWHATISMIND?

WHATISMATTER?NEVERMIND
HATISMATTER?NEVERMINDW
ATISMATTER?NEVERMINDWH
TISMATTER?NEVERMINDWHA
ISMATTER?NEVERMINDWHAT
SMATTER?NEVERMINDWHATI
MATTER?NEVERMINDWHATIS
ATTER?NEVERMINDWHATISM
TTER?NEVERMINDWHATISMA
TER?NEVERMINDWHATISMAT
ER?NEVERMINDWHATISMATT
R?NEVERMINDWHATISMATTE
?NEVERMINDWHATISMATTER
NEVERMINDWHATISMATTER?

¶WORDS MAY CHANGE THEIR MEANING. THE ONE THAT IS THE TITLE OF THIS ARTICLE MAY SERVE AS AN EXAMPLE. IT USED TO MEAN A PHILOSOPHICAL TENDENCY TO DENY THE REALITY OF MATTER (FOR INSTANCE BERKELEY). IT NOW OFTEN MEANS A FORM OF ART THAT RESULTS IN IMAGES WITHOUT MATERIAL SUPPORT (FOR INSTANCE HOLOGRAMS). BUT THERE MUST BE SOMETHING IN COMMON TO THOSE TWO MEANINGS. IF NOT, WHY USE THE SAME WORD? IT MUST BE POSSIBLE TO EXTIRPATE THAT COMMON NUCLEUS OUT FROM THOSE TWO WIDELY DIFFERENT MEANINGS. AND THAT NUCLEUS WILL HAVE SOMETHING TO DO WITH THE CONCEPT »MATTER«. NOW IF ONE SUCCEEDED IN DOING THIS, ONE WOULD HAVE OPENED AN ACCESS TO THE UNDERSTANDING OF THE CULTURAL REVOLUTION WE ARE WITNESSING. BECAUSE »MATTER« IS OBVIOUSLY A BASIC CONCEPT OF OUR CULTURE, AND IF IT HAS SHIFTED ITS MEANING, THE ENTIRE EDIFICE OF CULTURE WILL BE SHAKEN. THIS ARTICLE WILL EXAMINE THIS SHIFT. ¶CONCEPTS MUST BE DEFINED, IF THEY ARE TO HAVE A MEANING. THEY MUST BE DISTINGUISHED FROM OTHER CONCEPTS. FOR INSTANCE: THE CONCEPT »TABLE« CAN BE DEFINED

BY DISTINGUISHING IT FROM THE CONCEPT »CHAIR«. IT THEN BECOMES OPERATIVE. ONE MAY, FOR INSTANCE, CONSTRUCT A WIDER CONCEPT, NAMELY »FURNITURE«, AND HAVE IT COVER THE TWO ORIGINAL CONCEPTS. OR ONE MAY CONSTRUCT A GREY ZONE BETWEEN »TABLE« AND »CHAIR«, IN WHICH BOTH CONCEPTS APPLY, AND ONE MAY INSTALL, FOR INSTANCE, A SPECIFIC SORT OF SCHOOL FURNITURE WITHIN THAT GREY ZONE. NOW WITH THE CONCEPT »MATTER« THOSE OPERATIONS WILL NOT WORK, AND FOR A CURIOUS REASON. OUR TRADITION DEFINES »MATTER« WITH REGARD TO TWO OTHER CONCEPTS, NAMELY »SPIRIT« AND »FORM«. BUT IT DOES SO »DIALECTICALLY«, MEANING THAT THE TWO CONCEPTS DEFINED WITH REGARD TO EACH OTHER CONTRADICT EACH OTHER. THUS, »MATTER« IS EITHER DEFINED AS »OBJECT OF SPIRIT« OR AS »CONTENTS OF FORM«, AND, INVERSELY, »SPIRIT« IS DEFINED AS »THE SUBJECT OF MATTER« AND »FORM« IS DEFINED AS »CONTAINER OF MATTER«. NOW SUCH NEGATIVE DEFINITIONS DO NOT PERMIT OPERATIONS. NEITHER A WIDER CONCEPT, NOR A GREY ZONE BETWEEN CONCEPTS CAN BE CONSTRUCTED. IT

MATTERRETTAM
ATTERRETTAMM
TTERRETTAMMA
TERRETTAMMAT
ERRETTAMMATT
RRETTAMMATTE
RETTAMMATTER
ETTAMMATTERR
TTAMMATTERRE
TAMMATTERRET
AMMATTERRETT
MMATTERRETTA
MATTERRETTAM
MATTERRETTAM
ATTERRETTAMM
TTERRETTAMMA
TERRETTAMMAT
ERRETTAMMATT
RRETTAMMATTE
RETTAMMATTER
ETTAMMATTERR
TTAMMATTERRE
TAMMATTERRET
AMMATTERRETT
MMATTERRETTA
MATTERRETTAM

SPIRIT SPIRIT
S PIRIT SPIRI T
S P IRIT SPIR I T
S P I RIT SPI R I T
S P I R IT SP I R I T
S P I R I T S P I R I T
S P I R IT SP I R I T
S P I RIT SPI R I T
S PIRIT SPIRI T
SPIRIT SPIRIT
S PIRIT SPIRI T
S P IRIT SPIR I T
S P I RIT SPI R I T
S P I R IT SP I R I T
S P I R I T S P I R I T
S P I R IT SP I R I T
S P I RIT SPI R I T
S PIRIT SPIRI T
SPIRIT SPIRIT
S PIRIT SPIRI T
S P IRIT SPIR I T
S P I RIT SPI R I T
S P I R IT SP I R I T
S P I R I T S P I R I T
S P I R IT SP I R I T
S P I RIT SPI R I T
S PIRIT SPIRI T
SPIRIT SPIRIT

IS AS IF WE HAD DEFINED »TABLE« AS AN »ANTI-CHAIR« AND »CHAIR« AS AN »ANTI-TABLE«. THIS TYPE OF CLUMSY CONCEPT IS CALLED »METAPHYSICAL«, AND ALTHOUGH IT MIGHT BE ELEGANT IT IS NOT VERY USEFUL. ¶NON-WESTERN CULTURES DO NOT SEEM TO BE TROUBLED WITH THIS SORT OF METAPHYSICAL SCRUPLE, AS FAR AS THE CONCEPT »MATTER« IS CONCERNED. FOR INSTANCE, THEY QUITE HAPPILY CONSTRUCT A GREY ZONE BETWEEN »MATTER« AND »SPIRIT«, WHICH THEY FILL WITH THIN MATTER OR THICK SPIRIT OF THE TYPE »GHOST«, OR »ANGEL«, OR »ASTRAL BODY«, AND THEY EVEN PHOTOGRAPH THOSE PHANTOMS. OF COURSE: THIS INTERMEDIATE POPULATION EXISTS IN THE WEST JUST AS WELL AS ELSEWHERE, BUT WITH US IT IS CONSIDERED EITHER AS A REMNANT OF A PRIMITIVE AND ALMOST EXTINCT RACE, OR AS ILLEGAL IMMIGRATION. BECAUSE WE, THE TRUE HEIRS TO THE ANCIENT JEWS AND GREEKS, DO NOT PERMIT ANY SPIRITUALISATION OF MATTER OR MATERIALISATION OF SPIRIT. FOR US, THESE ARE OPPOSITE CONCEPTS, AND AN ABYSS SEPARATES THEM. ¶YES, BUT: IF »SPIRIT« MEANS »SUBJECT (OF MATTER)« AND »MATTER« MEANS

M
S M V
I S M V S
L I S M V S I
A L I S M V S I D
I A L I S M V S I D E
R I A L I S M V S I D E A
E R I A L I S M V S I D E A L
T E R I A L I S M V S I D E A L I
A T E R I A L I S M V S I D E A L I S
M A T E R I A L I S M V S I D E A L I S M
M A T E R I A L I S M V S I D E A L I S M
M A T E R I A L I S M V S I D E A L I S M
M A T E R I A L I S M V S I D E A L I S M
M A T E R I A L I S M V S I D E A L I S M
M A T E R I A L I S M V S I D E A L I S M
M A T E R I A L I S M V S I D E A L I S M
M A T E R I A L I S M V S I D E A L I S M
M A T E R I A L I S M V S I D E A L I S M
M A T E R I A L I S M V S I D E A L I S M
M A T E R I A L I S M V S I D E A L I S M
M A T E R I A L I S M V S I D E A L I S M
M A T E R I A L I S M V S I D E A L I S M
M A T E R I A L I S M V S I D E A L I S M
M A T E R I A L I S M V S I D E A L I S M
M A T E R I A L I S M V S I D E A L I S M
M A T E R I A L I S M V S I D E A L I S M
M A T E R I A L I S M V S I D E A L I S M
M A T E R I A L I S M V S I D E A L I S M
M A T E R I A L I S M V S I D E A L I S M
M A T E R I A L I S M V S I D E A L I S M
A T E R I A L I S M V S I D E A L I S
T E R I A L I S M V S I D E A L I
E R I A L I S M V S I D E A L
R I A L I S M V S I D E A
I A L I S M V S I D E
A L I S M V S I D
L I S M V S I
I S M V S
S M V
M

MATERIALISMVSIDEALISM
ATERIALISMVSIDEALISMM
TERIALISMVSIDEALISMMA
ERIALISMVSIDEALISMMAT
RIALISMVSIDEALISMMATE
IALISMVSIDEALISMMATER
ALISMVSIDEALISMMATERI
LISMVSIDEALISMMATERIA
ISMVSIDEALISMMATERIAL
SMVSIDEALISMMATERIALI
MVSIDEALISMMATERIALIS
VSIDEALISMMATERIALISM
SIDEALISMMATERIALISMV
IDEALISMMATERIALISMVS
DEALISMMATERIALISMVSI
EALISMMATERIALISMVSID
ALISMMATERIALISMVSIDE
LISMMATERIALISMVSIDEA
ISMMATERIALISMVSIDEAL
SMMATERIALISMVSIDEALI
MMATERIALISMVSIDEALIM
MATERIALISMVSIDEALIMM
ATERIALISMVSIDEALISMM
TERIALISMVSIDEALISMMA
ERIALISMVSIDEALISMMAT
RIALISMVSIDEALISMMATE
IALISMVSIDEALISMMATER
ALISMVSIDEALISMMATERI
LISMVSIDEALISMMATERIA
ISMVSIDEALISMMATERIAL
SMVSIDEALISMMATERIALI
MVSIDEALISMMATERIALIS
VSIDEALISMMATERIALISM
SIDEALISMMATERIALISMV
IDEALISMMATERIALISMVS
DEALISMMATERIALISMVSI
EALISMMATERIALISMVSID
ALISMMATERIALISMVSIDE
LISMMATERIALISMVSIDEA
ISMMATERIALISMVSIDEAL
SMMATERIALISMVSIDEALI
MMATERIALISMVSIDEALIM
MATERIALISMVSIDEALIMM

»OBJECT (OF SPIRIT)«, WHAT HAPPENS IF I THINK ABOUT »SPIRIT«? DOES IT NOT BECOME AN »OBJECT«, AND THUS A CURIOUS KIND OF »MATTER«? FOR INSTANCE, AS WITH DESCARTES, A »*RES COGITANS*«, A »THINKING THING«? AND, BEING A »THING«, MUST IT NOT BE LOCATED SOMEHOW SOMEWHERE, AT SOME MOMENT? THIS OF COURSE WOULD RESULT IN SUCH FUNNY PROBLEMS AS THE ONE THAT SEARCHES FOR THE »SEAT OF THE SOUL«. AND IF ONE PURSUES THIS QUEST FURTHER INTO THE DIRECTION OF ELEGANT SPIRITISM, ONE WILL FINALLY COME UP AGAINST THAT EVEN FUNNIER PROBLEM CONCERNING THE »IMMORTALITY OF THE SOUL«.

¶AN EVEN MORE IMPRESSIVE EXAMPLE FOR THE TROUBLES WE ARE IN WHEN TRYING TO OPERATE WITH THE CONCEPT »MATTER«: »SPIRIT« CONTRADICTS »MATTER« AND THIS CONTRADICTION MANIFESTS ITSELF AS »WORK«. THE RESULT OF THIS IS »CULTURE«. THEREFORE, CULTURAL OBJECTS ARE MATERIALISED SPIRIT AND SPIRITUALISED MATTER, ALTHOUGH NOT QUITE IN THE SENSE THAT EXTRA-OCCIDENTALS MEAN WHEN TALKING OF PHANTOMS, WHICH SHOWS THAT

METAPHYSICAL CONCEPTS ARE NOT VERY COMFORTABLE. ¶OF COURSE: THIS GORDIAN KNOT MAY BE EASILY CUT THROUGH, EITHER BY DENYING THE »REALITY« OF »MATTER« (IMMATERIALISM IN THE OLD SENSE) OR OF »SPIRIT« (RADICAL MATERIALISM). BUT THIS IS NOT A VERY CLEVER METHOD. IT LEAVES »MATTER« AND »SPIRIT« UNDEFINED, AND THUS WITHOUT MEANING. TO SAY THAT »EVERYTHING IS MATTER (OR SPIRIT)« IS JUST AS MEANINGFUL AS IS A COCK'S CROWING. WE MUST FIND OTHER WAYS OUT, AND SCIENCE IS TRYING TO DO SO. ¶SCIENCE DEVELOPED FROM PHILOSOPHY LIKE A BUTTERFLY FROM ITS COCOON, AND WHAT I HAVE DISCUSSED UP TO THIS POINT IS THAT EMPTY SHELL, WHICH SCIENCE HAS LEFT BEHIND. NONETHELESS, SCIENCE COULD NOT BUT INHERIT THE CONCEPT »MATTER« FROM PHILOSOPHY, BECAUSE THIS IS A BASIC CONCEPT. AND IT DID NOT KNOW VERY WELL WHAT TO DO WITH THIS CLUMSY CONCEPT, EXCEPT TO TRY AND MEASURE IT. THUS, IT INVENTED THE CONCEPT »MASS«, WHICH IS ALSO NOT VERY COMFORTABLE, BUT WHICH AT LEAST PERMITS ONE TO POSE THE QUESTION OF THE STRUCTURE OF MATTER. THE RESULT, ALTHOUGH NOT VERY HELPFUL, IF

THE OVERCOMING OF METAPHYSICS IS THE AIM, IS, TO SAY THE LEAST, SURPRISING. ¶»MATTER« NOW LOOKS VERY MUCH LIKE A SERIES OF RUSSIAN DOLLS, ONE CONTAINING THE OTHERS. THE BIGGEST DOLL IS ASTRONOMICAL (EINSTEINIAN), IT CONTAINS THE MOLECULAR DOLL (NEWTONIAN), WHICH CONTAINS THE ATOMIC DOLL (WHERE MASS AND ENERGY MERGE), WHICH AGAIN CONTAINS THE NUCLEAR DOLL (WHERE CAUSALITY ABDICATES IN FAVOUR OF STATISTICS), WHICH AGAIN CONTAINS THE PARTICLE DOLL (WHICH POSES CURIOUS PROBLEMS OF SYMMETRY) AND THE SMALLEST DOLL IS THE QUARK DOLL (WHERE IT IS DIFFICULT, EVEN MEANINGLESS, TO DISTINGUISH BETWEEN PHENOMENON AND MATHEMATICAL SYMBOL). NOW THIS DOES NOT SOUND VERY HELPFUL, EXCEPT FOR ONE BIG SURPRISE, WHICH IS THAT WHATEVER PHILOSOPHY SAYS CONCERNING »MATTER« RELATES EXCLUSIVELY TO THE MOLECULAR LEVEL. ON ALL OTHER LEVELS, IT IS NONSENSE TO SAY THAT »MATTER« IS AN »OBJECT OF SPIRIT« OR A »CONTENT OF FORM«. ¶THUS, ALL OF THE ETERNAL PROBLEMS THAT PHILOSOPHY HAS WITH MATTER, LIKE THE

HY
PHYS
APHYSI
TAPHYSIC
ETAPHYSICA
METAPHYSICAL
M ETAPHYSICA L
M E TAPHYSIC A L
M E T APHYSI C A L
M E T A PHYS I C A L
M E T A P HY S I C A L
M E T A PHYS I C A L
M E T APHYSI C A L
M E TAPHYSIC A L
M ETAPHYSICA L
METAPHYSICAL
ETAPHYSICA
TAPHYSIC
APHYSI
PHYS
HY

D I A L E C T I C
D I A L E C T I C A
D I A L E C T I C A L
D I A L E C T I C A L L
D I A L E C T I C A L L Y
D I A L E C T I C A L L Y O
D I A L E C T I C A L L Y O P
D I A L E C T I C A L L Y O P P
D I A L E C T I C A L L Y O P P O
D I A L E C T I C A L L Y O P P O S
D I A L E C T I C A L L Y O P P O S E
D I A L E C T I C A L L Y O P P O S E D
D I A L E C T I C A L L Y O P P O S E
D I A L E C T I C A L L Y O P P O S
D I A L E C T I C A L L Y O P P O
D I A L E C T I C A L L Y O P P
D I A L E C T I C A L L Y O P
D I A L E C T I C A L L Y O
D I A L E C T I C A L L Y
D I A L E C T I C A L L
D I A L E C T I C A L
D I A L E C T I C A
D I A L E C T I C

PROBLEM OF THE IMMORTALITY OF THE SOUL OR THE MATERIALISATION OF THE SPIRIT THROUGH COMMITMENT TO CULTURE, ARE SHOWN TO BE MOLECULAR PROBLEMS. AT FIRST SIGHT, THIS DOES NOT SOUND VERY STUNNING. DO WE NOT LIVE ON THE MOLECULAR LEVEL, ITS DIMENSIONS BEING OURS (OUR BODIES ARE MEASURED IN CENTIMETRES, AND OUR AGE IN SECONDS)? ALL THE OTHER LEVELS OF MATTER ARE EXISTENTIALLY IMMEASURABLE FOR US, AND DO NOT CONCERN US. THE ETERNAL PROBLEMS OF PHILOSOPHY ARE THUS OUR PROBLEMS, AND NOTHING SCIENCE MAY SAY CAN CHANGE THIS. SCIENCE IS INCOMPETENT IN THE FACE OF THIS KIND OF PROBLEM.

¶AT SECOND SIGHT, HOWEVER, THIS BECOMES UNTRUE. WE DO NOT LIVE EXCLUSIVELY WITHIN THE CENTIMETRE/SECOND DIMENSION. PROCESSES GO ON WITHIN OUR BRAIN AND OUR NERVOUS SYSTEM, WHICH HAVE ALTOGETHER DIFFERENT DIMENSIONS. PARTICLES ENTER THOSE SYSTEMS, THEY JUMP QUANTICALLY BETWEEN THE NERVE SYNAPSES, AND THEY ARE PROCESSED THERE. AND WE EXPERIENCE THIS AS PERCEPTION, IMAGINATION, WISHING, THOUGHT, AND DECISION MAKING. WE LIVE CONCRETELY JUST AS

SPIRITUALISEDMATTER
PIRITUALISEDMATTERS
IRITUALISEDMATTERSP
RITUALISEDMATTERSPI
ITUALISEDMATTERSPIR
TUALISEDMATTERSPIRI
UALISEDMATTERSPIRIT
ALISEDMATTERSPIRITU
LISEDMATTERSPIRITUA
ISEDMATTERSPIRITUAL
SEDMATTERSPIRITUALI
EDMATTERSPIRITUALIS
DMATTERSPIRITUALISE
MATTERSPIRITUALISED
ATTERSPIRITUALISEDM
TTERSPIRITUALISEDMA
TERSPIRITUALISEDMAT
ERSPIRITUALISEDMATT
RSPIRITUALISEDMATTE
SPIRITUALISEDMATTER
PIRITUALISEDMATTERS
IRITUALISEDMATTERSP
RITUALISEDMATTERSPI
ITUALISEDMATTERSPIR
TUALISEDMATTERSPIRI
UALISEDMATTERSPIRIT
ALISEDMATTERSPIRITU
LISEDMATTERSPIRITUA
ISEDMATTERSPIRITUAL
SEDMATTERSPIRITUALI
EDMATTERSPIRITUALIS
DMATTERSPIRITUALISE
MATTERSPIRITUALISED
ATTERSPIRITUALISEDM
TTERSPIRITUALISEDMA
TERSPIRITUALISEDMAT
ERSPIRITUALISEDMATT
RSPIRITUALISEDMATTE
SPIRITUALISEDMATTER

MATERIALISEDSPIRIT
ATERIALISEDSPIRITM
TERIALISEDSPIRITMA
ERIALISEDSPIRITMAT
RIALISEDSPIRITMATE
IALISEDSPIRITMATER
ALISEDSPIRITMATERI
LISEDSPIRITMATERIA
ISEDSPIRITMATERIAL
SEDSPIRITMATERIALI
EDSPIRITMATERIALIS
DSPIRITMATERIALISE
SPIRITMATERIALISED
PIRITMATERIALISEDS
IRITMATERIALISEDSP
RITMATERIALISEDSPI
ITMATERIALISEDSPIR
TMATERIALISEDSPIRI
MATERIALISEDSPIRIT
MATERIALISEDSPIRIT
ATERIALISEDSPIRITM
TERIALISEDSPIRITMA
ERIALISEDSPIRITMAT
RIALISEDSPIRITMATE
IALISEDSPIRITMATER
ALISEDSPIRITMATERI
LISEDSPIRITMATERIA
ISEDSPIRITMATERIAL
SEDSPIRITMATERIALI
EDSPIRITMATERIALIS
DSPIRITMATERIALISE
SPIRITMATERIALISED
PIRITMATERIALISEDS
IRITMATERIALISEDSP
RITMATERIALISEDSPI
ITMATERIALISEDSPIR
TMATERIALISEDSPIRI
MATERIALISEDSPIRIT

MUCH ON THE LEVELS OF PARTICLES AS WE LIVE ON THE MOLECULAR LEVEL, WHICH GIVES RISE TO A CURIOUS SUSPICION: WHAT IF »SPIRIT« WERE THE NAME WE GIVE »MATTER« ON THE LEVEL OF PARTICLES, AND WHAT IF »MATTER« WERE THE NAME WE GIVE »SPIRIT« IN THE MOLECULAR LEVEL? THIS MIGHT NOT SOUND LIKE A VERY ORIGINAL SUSPICION (IT SOUNDS LIKE SPIRITISM) BUT, UNLIKE SPIRITISM, IT PERMITS TECHNICAL EXPERIMENTATION. ¶UNTIL RECENTLY, ALL EXPEDITIONS UNDERTAKEN INTO THE VARIOUS LEVELS OF MATTER STARTED FROM THE MOLECULAR LEVEL. DEMOCRITUS LEFT IT IN SEARCH OF ATOMS, ARISTOTLE IN SEARCH OF THE STARS AND SCIENCE CONTINUED TO DO SO, ALTHOUGH IT ORGANISED ITS EXPEDITIONS A LITTLE BIT MORE CAREFULLY. THIS IS CHANGING. WE NOW WITNESS EXPEDITIONS COMING FROM THE LEVEL OF PARTICLES THAT INVADE THE MOLECULAR LEVEL AS IF FROM BELOW. THINGS LIKE THERMONUCLEAR POWER STATIONS, COMPUTERS, ROBOTS, OR ELECTROMAGNETIC IMAGES ARE PARTICLES INVADING OUR MOLECULAR LEVEL. THEY EXPLODE OUR ETERNAL PROBLEMS. IT IS NONSENSE TO SAY OF A

THERMONUCLEAR PLANT THAT IT SPIRITUALISES MATTER; OF A COMPUTER, THAT IT IS A MATERIALISED SPIRIT; OF A ROBOT, THAT IT DECIDES AND ACTS UPON DECISIONS; OR OF A TV IMAGE THAT IT IS A PURE, PLATONIC FORM. ALL SUCH METAPHYSICAL FORMULATIONS FAIL, WHERE SUCH PARTICLE INVASIONS ARE CONCERNED. INSTEAD, IT BECOMES POSSIBLE TO EXPERIMENT WITH THESE SORTS OF PROCESSES, WHICH ARE OF THE ORDER OF MAGNITUDE OUR BRAIN INHABITS. ¶SO-CALLED »ARTIFICIAL INTELLIGENCES« MAY SERVE AS EXAMPLES FOR THIS TRANSITION FROM METAPHYSICS TO TECHNICAL EXPERIMENTATION. THEY ARE RUDIMENTARY SIMULATIONS OF A FEW BRAIN FUNCTIONS. NEUROPHYSIOLOGY HAS NOT ADVANCED VERY FAR INTO THE SECRETS OF THE BRAIN, BUT FAR ENOUGH TO PERMIT THOSE SIMULATIONS. THIS IS NOT SURPRISING: PALAEOLITHIC MAN DID NOT NEED A WELL-ELABORATED THEORY OF MECHANICS TO SIMULATE A FEW FUNCTIONS OF HIS ARM TO INVENT THE LEVER. OF COURSE: IT WOULD BE AN EXAGGERATION TO CALL A LEVER AN »ARTIFICIAL ARM«, JUST AS IT IS AN EXAGGERATION TO CALL OUR CRUDE SIMULATION

M A T T E R OBJECTOFSPIRIT
M A T T E R :OBJECTOFSPIRI T
M A T T E R:OBJECTOFSPIR I T
M A T T ER:OBJECTOFSPI R I T
M A T TER:OBJECTOFSP I R I T
M A TTER:OBJECTOFS P I R I T
M ATTER:OBJECTOF S P I R I T
MATTER:OBJECTO F S P I R I T
M ATTER:OBJECT O F S P I R I T
M A TTER:OBJEC T O F S P I R I T
M A T TER:OBJE C T O F S P I R I T
M A T T ER:OBJ E C T O F S P I R I T
M A T T E R:OB J E C T O F S P I R I T
M A T T E R :O B J E C T O F S P I R I T
M A T T E R:OB J E C T O F S P I R I T
M A T T ER:OBJ E C T O F S P I R I T
M A T TER:OBJE C T O F S P I R I T
M A TTER:OBJEC T O F S P I R I T
M ATTER:OBJECT O F S P I R I T
MATTER:OBJECTO F S P I R I T
M ATTER:OBJECTOF S P I R I T
M A TTER:OBJECTOFS P I R I T
M A T TER:OBJECTOFSP I R I T
M A T T ER:OBJECTOFSPI R I T
M A T T E R:OBJECTOFSPIR I T
M A T T E R :OBJECTOFSPIRI T
M A T T E R OBJECTOFSPIRIT

S P I R I T   SUBJECTOFMATTER
S P I R I T : SUBJECTOFMATTE R
S P I R I T: SUBJECTOFMATT E R
S P I R IT: SUBJECTOFMAT T E R
S P I RIT: SUBJECTOFMA T T E R
S P IRIT: SUBJECTOFM A T T E R
S PIRIT: SUBJECTOF M A T T E R
SPIRIT: SUBJECTO F M A T T E R
S PIRIT: SUBJECT O F M A T T E R
S P IRIT: SUBJEC T O F M A T T E R
S P I RIT: SUBJE C T O F M A T T E R
S P I R IT: SUBJ E C T O F M A T T E R
S P I R I T: SUB J E C T O F M A T T E R
S P I R I T : SU B J E C T O F M A T T E R
S P I R I T : S U B J E C T O F M A T T E R
S P I R I T : SU B J E C T O F M A T T E R
S P I R I T: SUB J E C T O F M A T T E R
S P I R IT: SUBJ E C T O F M A T T E R
S P I RIT: SUBJE C T O F M A T T E R
S P IRIT: SUBJEC T O F M A T T E R
S PIRIT: SUBJECT O F M A T T E R
SPIRIT: SUBJECTO F M A T T E R
S PIRIT: SUBJECTOF M A T T E R
S P IRIT: SUBJECTOFM A T T E R
S P I RIT: SUBJECTOFMA T T E R
S P I R IT: SUBJECTOFMAT T E R
S P I R I T: SUBJECTOFMATT E R
S P I R I T : SUBJECTOFMATTE R
S P I R I T   SUBJECTOFMATTER

OF BRAINS »ARTIFICIAL INTELLIGENCES«. STILL, THE LEVER IS THE ANCESTOR OF ALL MACHINES, AND MACHINES HAVE NOT ONLY TAKEN OVER MOST OF THE MUSCULAR BODY FUNCTIONS, THEY HAVE EXCEEDED THE MECHANICAL CAPACITIES OF THE BODY BY A LONG WAY. WE ARE, AS FAR AS OUR INTELLECTUAL CAPACITIES ARE CONCERNED, AT THE STAGE OF THE LEVER. ¶NOW THESE CRUDE SIMULATIONS SHOW THAT MUCH OF WHAT PHILOSOPHY (AND THEOLOGY) USED TO CONSIDER »SPIRIT« (LIKE LOGICAL REASONING OR DECISION MAKING) CAN BE PERFORMED BY APPARATUS. THUS, »SPIRIT« IS BEGINNING TO ESCAPE FROM ITS IMPRISONMENT WITHIN THE SKULL, AND MAY BE OBSERVED AS IF FROM OUTSIDE. THE FOGS OF PHILOSOPHY, THEOLOGY, PSYCHOLOGY, AND OTHER IDEOLOGIES THAT ENVELOP IT ARE LIFTING. WE SHALL HAVE TO THINK EVERYTHING CONCERNING »SPIRIT« ALL OVER AGAIN. ¶ANOTHER SUCH INVASION OF PARTICLES INTO THE MOLECULAR LEVEL IS ELECTROMAGNETIC IMAGES, AND THEY TOO OBLIGE US TO RETHINK ETERNAL PROBLEMS. BUT WITH THEM, IT IS NOT THE DIALECTICS OF »MATTER-SPIRIT« THAT

ARE IN QUESTION, BUT THE DIALECTICS »MATTER-FORM«: LET US CONSIDER IT. ¶THERE IS A CURIOUS MYTH THAT SUSTAINS WESTERN THOUGHT IN THIS RESPECT, AND WHAT IT SAYS IS THIS: IN THE BEGINNING (WHATEVER THAT MAY MEAN), THERE WAS A FORMLESS SOUP CALLED »MATTER« AND OVER IT HOVERED EMPTY FORMS (SOMETIMES CALLED »IDEAS«). THE FORMS SOMEHOW DIPPED INTO MATTER LIKE SPOONS AND FILLED THEMSELVES, AND THIS IS CALLED »CREATION«. NOW, ALTHOUGH THIS MYTH IS UNBELIEVABLE, IT IS DEEPLY ROOTED IN US. WERE WE TO GIVE IT UP, WE WOULD HAVE GIVEN UP JUDEO-CHRISTIANITY AND THE GREEK BELIEF THAT THE UNIVERSE HAS A MATHEMATICAL STRUCTURE. WE WOULD ALSO HAVE TO GIVE UP THE ENDLESS QUARREL BETWEEN »MATERIALISM« AND »IDEALISM«. BUT WE WILL HAVE TO GIVE IT UP IN THE FACE OF SCIENCE. ¶SCIENCE SAYS THAT THE UNIVERSE IS A PROCESS, OR AN EVER MORE UNIFORM DISTRIBUTION OF THE PARTICLES FROM WHICH IT IS COMPOSED. IT TENDS TOWARDS THE TOTAL LOSS OF FORM. IN FACT, THIS TENDENCY TOWARDS LOSS OF FORM MAY BE TAKEN AS

ARTIFICIALI N T E L L I G E N C E
A RTIFICIALIN T E L L I G E N C E
A R TIFICIALINT E L L I G E N C E
A R T IFICIALINTE L L I G E N C E
A R T I FICIALINTEL L I G E N C E
A R T I F ICIALINTELL I G E N C E
A R T I F I CIALINTELLI G E N C E
A R T I F I C IALINTELLIG E N C E
A R T I F I C I ALINTELLIGE N C E
A R T I F I C I A LINTELLIGEN C E
A R T I F I C I A L INTELLIGENC E
A R T I F I C I A LINTELLIGEN C E
A R T I F I C I ALINTELLIGE N C E
A R T I F I C IALINTELLIG E N C E
A R T I F I CIALINTELLI G E N C E
A R T I F ICIALINTELL I G E N C E
A R T I FICIALINTEL L I G E N C E
A R T IFICIALINTE L L I G E N C E
A R TIFICIALINT E L L I G E N C E
A RTIFICIALIN T E L L I G E N C E
ARTIFICIALI N T E L L I G E N C E
A RTIFICIALIN T E L L I G E N C E
A R TIFICIALINT E L L I G E N C E
A R T IFICIALINTE L L I G E N C E
A R T I FICIALINTEL L I G E N C E
A R T I F ICIALINTELL I G E N C E
A R T I F I CIALINTELLI G E N C E
A R T I F I C IALINTELLIG E N C E
A R T I F I C I ALINTELLIGE N C E
A R T I F I C I A LINTELLIGEN C E
A R T I F I C I A L INTELLIGENC E
A R T I F I C I A LINTELLIGEN C E
A R T I F I C I ALINTELLIGE N C E
A R T I F I C IALINTELLIG E N C E
A R T I F I CIALINTELLI G E N C E
A R T I F ICIALINTELL I G E N C E
A R T I FICIALINTEL L I G E N C E
A R T IFICIALINTE L L I G E N C E
A R TIFICIALINT E L L I G E N C E
A RTIFICIALIN T E L L I G E N C E
ARTIFICIALI N T E L L I G E N C E

A R T I F I C I A L I N
A   R T I F I C I A L I N T
A   R   T I F I C I A L I N T E
A   R   T   I F I C I A L I N T E L
A   R   T   I   F I C I A L I N T E L L
A   R   T   I   F   I C I A L I N T E L L I
A   R   T   I   F   I   C I A L I N T E L L I G
A   R   T   I   F   I   C   I A L I N T E L L I G E
A   R   T   I   F   I   C   I   A L I N T E L L I G E N
A   R   T   I   F   I   C   I   A   L I N T E L L I G E N C
A   R   T   I   F   I   C   I   A   L   I N T E L L I G E N C E
A   R   T   I   F   I   C   I   A   L I N T E L L I G E N C
A   R   T   I   F   I   C   I   A L I N T E L L I G E N
A   R   T   I   F   I   C   I A L I N T E L L I G E
A   R   T   I   F   I   C I A L I N T E L L I G
A   R   T   I   F   I C I A L I N T E L L I
A   R   T   I   F I C I A L I N T E L L
A   R   T   I F I C I A L I N T E L
A   R   T I F I C I A L I N T E
A   R T I F I C I A L I N T
A R T I F I C I A L I N T E L L I G E N C E
I N T E L L I G E N C   E
L I N T E L L I G E N   C   E
A L I N T E L L I G E   N   C   E
I A L I N T E L L I G   E   N   C   E
C I A L I N T E L L I   G   E   N   C   E
I C I A L I N T E L L   I   G   E   N   C   E
F I C I A L I N T E L   L   I   G   E   N   C   E
I F I C I A L I N T E   L   L   I   G   E   N   C   E
T I F I C I A L I N T   E   L   L   I   G   E   N   C   E
R T I F I C I A L I N   T   E   L   L   I   G   E   N   C   E
A R T I F I C I A L I   N   T   E   L   L   I   G   E   N   C   E
R T I F I C I A L I N   T   E   L   L   I   G   E   N   C   E
T I F I C I A L I N T   E   L   L   I   G   E   N   C   E
I F I C I A L I N T E   L   L   I   G   E   N   C   E
F I C I A L I N T E L   L   I   G   E   N   C   E
I C I A L I N T E L L   I   G   E   N   C   E
C I A L I N T E L L I   G   E   N   C   E
I A L I N T E L L I G   E   N   C   E
A L I N T E L L I G E   N   C   E
L I N T E L L I G E N   C   E
I N T E L L I G E N C   E
N T E L L I G E N C E

A MEASURE OF THE AGE OF THE UNIVERSE AS A WHOLE, AND OF EVERY PHENOMENON THEREIN (E.G. THE CARBON TEST). THE EQUATIONS THAT PERMIT THIS MEASUREMENT ARE THOSE OF THE SECOND PRINCIPLE OF THERMODYNAMICS. ¶NOW, WHAT THOSE EQUATIONS MEAN IS THAT EVERYTHING TENDS TO BECOME MORE PROBABLE, AND THAT WHAT WE CALL THE »UNIVERSE« IS AN IMPROBABLE, TRANSITORY STAGE OF THIS PROCESS. THUS, WHAT WE CALL »MATTER« IS AN IMPROBABLE FORM OF ENERGY THAT WILL DECAY INTO UNIFORMLY DISTRIBUTED HEAT (THERMIC DEATH). THUS, »MATTER« AND »FORM« COME TO MEAN THE SAME THING, NAMELY A TRANSITORY AND IMPROBABLE STAGE OF ENERGY DISTRIBUTION. ¶WHAT IS SURPRISING IN THIS IS NOT SO MUCH THAT THE ANCIENT DIALECTICS OF »MATTER-FORM« HAS LOST ITS MEANING. RATHER, IT IS THE CENTRAL POSITION THAT THE CONCEPT »PROBABILITY« TAKES. IT HAS SOMETHING TO DO WITH GAMES, WITH CHANCE, WITH LUCK, WITH ACCIDENTS, IN SHORT: WITH DICE. THE UNIVERSE APPEARS AS A KIND OF BLIND GAME, WHICH WILL RESULT IN THE END IN THE EXHAUSTION OF ALL ITS CHANCES

PROBA B ILITY
ROBA B ILITYP
OBA B ILITYPR
BA B ILITYPRO
A B ILITYPROB
 B ILITYPROBA
B ILITYPROBA
 ILITYPROBA B
ILITYPROBA B
LITYPROBA B I
ITYPROBA B IL
TYPROBA B ILI
YPROBA B ILIT
PROBA B ILITY
ROBA B ILITYP
OBA B ILITYPR
BA B ILITYPRO
A B ILITYPROB
 B ILITYPROBA
B ILITYPROBA
 ILITYPROBA B
ILITYPROBA B
LITYPROBA B I
ITYPROBA B IL
TYPROBA B ILI
YPROBA B ILIT
PROBA B ILITY

SYNT H ESIS
YNT H ESISS
NT H ESISSY
T H ESISSYN
 H ESISSYNT
H ESISSYNT
 ESISSYNT H
ESISSYNT H
SISSYNT H E
ISSYNT H ES
SSYNT H ESI
SYNT H ESIS
YNT H ESISS
NT H ESISSY
T H ESISSYN
 H ESISSYNT
H ESISSYNT
 ESISSYNT H
ESISSYNT H
SISSYNT H E
ISSYNT H ES
SSYNT H ESI
SYNT H ESIS

(A ZERO-SUM GAME), BUT IN THE COURSE OF THIS ACCIDENTS MAY OCCUR, UNFORESEEABLE SITUATIONS. AND IT IS THESE ACCIDENTS, THESE STROKES OF LUCK, WHICH CONCENTRATE OUR ATTENTION. THE EQUATIONS OF THE SECOND PRINCIPLE OF THERMODYNAMICS, WHICH MEASURE THE TENDENCY TOWARDS THE EVER MORE PROBABLE, MAY BE TURNED AROUND, AND THEY WILL THEN POINT TOWARDS THE IMPROBABLE, THE ACCIDENTAL. THIS TURNING AROUND HAS BEEN ACHIEVED BY THE THEORY OF INFORMATION. AND ELECTROMAGNETIC IMAGES MAY BE CONSIDERED TO BE RESULTS OF THIS THEORETICAL UNDERSTANDING OF »INFORMATION«. ¶WHAT ONE SEES, IF ONE LOOKS AT IMAGES LIKE VIDEO-CLIPS, HOLOGRAMS, OR THOSE SYNTHESISED ON COMPUTER SCREENS IS HIGHLY IMPROBABLE CONFIGURATIONS OF PARTICLES LIKE PHOTONS. THESE IMPROBABLE CONFIGURATIONS HAVE NOT COME ABOUT BY BLIND CHANCE (AS THEY DO, FOR INSTANCE IN GENETIC INFORMATION), BUT BY HUMAN DELIBERATION. THEY ARE THE RESULT OF A DELIBERATE INVERSION OF THE UNIVERSAL TENDENCY TOWARDS UNIFORM

DISTRIBUTION. HE WHO PRODUCES THEM PLAYS WITH CHANCE AGAINST CHANCE; HE PLAYS AGAINST THE BLIND GAME OF »NATURE«. THIS MAY BE SEEN IN EVERY IMMATERIAL IMAGE, BUT WITH SYNTHETIC IMAGES THE STRATEGY USED (IN THIS GAME AGAINST THE GAME) IS CLEAREST: IT IS THE STRATEGY OF COMPUTATION. AND THIS IS PRECISELY WHAT THE TERM »IMMATERIALISM« HAS COME TO MEAN: A DELIBERATE PLAY WITH PARTICLES, SO THAT THEY MAY ACQUIRE IMPROBABLE FORMS; THAT THEY MAY BECOME »INFORMATION« USING THE STRATEGY OF COMPUTATION.

¶ONE MAY NOW TRY TO SEE HOW FAR THIS ARTICLE HAS SUCCEEDED IN UNCOVERING THE COMMON NUCLEUS OF THE TWO MEANINGS OF THE TERM »IMMATERIALISM«. WHEN FIRST USED, THE WORD STOOD IN A CULTURAL CONTEXT WHERE »MATTER« WAS EITHER DEFINED AS THE »OBJECT OF SPIRIT«, OR AS THE »CONTENTS OF FORMS«. THESE DEFINITIONS ARE NO LONGER USEFUL. AS IT IS NOW BEING USED, THE WORD STANDS IN A CULTURAL CONTEXT WHERE BOTH »MATTER« AND »SPIRIT« MUST BE THOUGHT OF AS IMPROBABLE »FORMS« OF WHAT MAY BE CALLED

¶STILL: FUTURE »IMMATERIAL« CULTURE, THE CULTURE OF »PURE INFORMATION« WILL BE ALMOST COMPLETELY DIFFERENT FROM OURS. AND THIS, IS WHAT IS SUGGESTED HERE BY THE SHIFT IN THE MEANING OF THE WORD »IMMATERIALISM«.

»ENERGY« (A TERM THAT DEFIES DEFINITION). NO DOUBT, HERE, WE HAVE COME UP AGAINST A PROFOUND CULTURAL REVOLUTION. THE VERY PILLARS OF WESTERN CULTURE, »MATTER«, »SPIRIT«, AND »FORM« HAVE FALLEN. BUT WE HAVE BY NO MEANS OVERCOME METAPHYSICS. WE HAVE DEMYSTIFIED THESE THREE PILLARS, BUT A MYSTERY NOW ENVELOPS THE CONCEPTS OF »ENERGY« AND »PROBABILITY« INSTEAD. IF ONE THROWS METAPHYSICS OUT THROUGH THE DOOR, IT COMES BACK THROUGH THE WINDOW.

M

M S M

M S I S M

M S I L I S M

M S I L A L I S M

M S I L A I A L I S M

M S I L A I R I A L I S M

M S I L A I R E R I A L I S M

M S I L A I R E T E R I A L I S M

M S I L A I R E T A T E R I A L I S M

M S I L A I R E T A M A T E R I A L I S M

M S I L A I R E T A M M M A T E R I A L I S M

M S I L A I R E T A M M I M M A T E R I A L I S M

M S I L A I R E T A M M M A T E R I A L I S M

M S I L A I R E T A M A T E R I A L I S M

M S I L A I R E T A T E R I A L I S M

M S I L A I R E T E R I A L I S M

M S I L A I R E R I A L I S M

M S I L A I R I A L I S M

M S I L A I A L I S M

M S I L A L I S M

M S I L I S M

M S I S M

M S M

M

www.ingramcontent.com/pod-product-compliance
Ingram Content Group UK Ltd.
Pitfield, Milton Keynes, MK11 3LW, UK
UKHW020418250726
13967UKWH00007B/2699

9 780993 327216